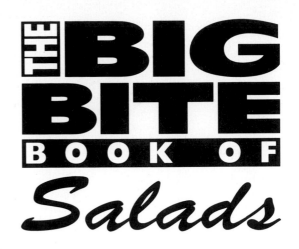

# THE BIG BITE BOOK OF
## *Salads*

# THE BIG BITE BOOK OF Salads

MEG JANSZ

SMITHMARK

This edition published in 1995 by
SMITHMARK Publishers Inc.,
16 East 32nd Street,
New York, NY 10016.

1 2 3 4 5 6 7 8 9

SMITHMARK books are available for bulk purchase
for sales promotion and premium use. For details
write or call the manager of special sales,
SMITHMARK Publishers Inc.,
16 East 32nd Street, New York,
NY 10016; (212) 532-6600

ISBN 0-8317-0759-3

Printed in Singapore

**CREDITS**
Author and home economist: Meg Jansz
Managing editor: Lisa Dyer
Photographer: Ken Field
Designer: Paul Johnson
Stylist: Marian Price
Filmset: SX Composing Ltd, England
Color Separation: P&W Graphics Pte, Ltd,
    Singapore

**Other titles of interest:**
The Big Bite Book of BARBECUES
The Big Bite Book of BURGERS
The Big Bite Book of PIZZAS

# CONTENTS

# INTRODUCTION

*The Big Bite Book of Salads* contains five chapters of varied salad recipes to suit all tastes and occasions. Along with substantial main-course salads, lighter salads for eating as first courses or on the side are also included, as well as a selection of fruit salads to round off a meal. All the serving sizes recommended in the recipes are for side salads, first courses or light lunches, unless otherwise indicated as main-course meals. Some of the recipes are adaptations of traditional salads, while others are innovative and totally original creations.

Every civilization has eaten some mixture of raw indigenous vegetables as a health-giving part of its diet. Salads were originally the edible parts of various herbs and plants seasoned only with salt – the Latin word "sāl," from which the word "salad" derives.

As time progressed, the composition of salads became more varied. As early as 1699 in England, John Evelyn's *Acetaria* described "Sallets" as "a composition of Edule Plants and Roots of several kinds, to be eaten raw or green, blanched or candied, simple and serfe, or intermingled with others according to the season." Evelyn recommended that the ingredients of a salad be carefully selected to complement and balance each other.

*Acetaria* distinguishes between simple and combined salads, however it is in classic French cooking where this distinction has evolved fully. French salads are traditionally of two types: a simple salad of tossed lettuce or another single vegetable, usually served after the main course, and a more complex combination salad, served as a separate hors d'oeuvre or even a light main course in itself.

It is the combination salad that has developed into the increasingly popular main-course salad, which now features extremely diverse ingredients, including meat, seafood, cheese, nuts and grains.

Although many salads contain these rather calorific ingredients, salads are fundamentally healthy because their basic ingredients are raw vegetables or fruits with their inherent vitamins and minerals intact.

## CHOOSING AND STORING INGREDIENTS

Using raw ingredients as the basis of your dish means that good quality is essential! For salad-making, always choose the best and freshest ingredients available. Although most fresh produce is now found, at a price, on supermarket shelves year-round, for quality and value buy produce during its growing season.

Fresh asparagus in spring, sun-ripened strawberries a little later on and crisp seasonal lettuce will always taste better than their forced greenhouse counterparts. The availability of root vegetables, grains, dried fruits and nuts in all seasons does enable you to make tasty salads throughout the year.

Once you have bought your ingredients, store them carefully. Salad vegetables should always be kept in a cool dark place, preferably in a refrigerator. This will keep them firm and fresh. Fresh herbs last best in the refrigerator, either sprayed with water and placed in a plastic bag or standing in bowls of water.

**RIGHT:** Look for the freshest ingredients for your salads: ripe fruits, crisp lettuces and herbs, and any unusual colors or varieties.

Nuts are an excellent source of fiber and add crunch to salads. However, their shelf-life is relatively short because they have a high oil content, and can turn rancid. Buy nuts in small quantities, store them in airtight containers, and use them quickly.

## DRESSINGS

Dressings are an integral part of any good salad. They should always work together with the tastes of the salad ingredients, without being overpowering.

In vinaigrette dressings, my personal ideal proportions are 3 parts oil to 1 part vinegar or citrus juice. However, you should experiment and alter proportions to suit your own tastes.

Many different oils are readily available. The most popular, olive oil, is used in many classic European recipes and is a monounsaturate, generally accepted as lower in cholesterol than, for example, the more exotic nut oils. For the health-conscious, use light olive oil.

The dressings in this book use traditional oils, such as olive and sunflower, as well as more unusual newcomers, such as hazelnut, walnut, chili and sesame oils. You may like to prepare your own flavored oils by adding some dried chilies, garlic, or herb sprigs to a bottle of oil. If you do this, allow the flavors to develop for at least two weeks.

## PREPARATION

Always ensure that all vegetables are washed before using. Washed salad leaves should be dried before dressing is added. The leaves will be crisper and the dressing will coat the leaves as well. The best and quickest way to dry leaves is in a salad spinner, but a clean, dry dish towel can also be used to pat leaves dry.

If using nuts, toast them in advance, as this enhances their flavor. Dressings can also be made in advance and set aside for their flavors to develop and create a stronger taste. However, dressings should be added to the salad just before serving to prevent leaves from becoming soggy. An exception is with pasta, grain and rice salads, where adding the dressings to the warm, cooked base ingredient allows the ingredients to absorb the flavors without affecting the look of the salad.

## PRESENTING YOUR SALAD

The visual appeal of food is a vital part of its enjoyment, so it is worth spending time on attractive presentation. Even the simplest side salad can be made decorative by careful slicing, an imaginative combination of colors, and the arrangement of the ingredients on the plate. Not all salads need to be tossed; you can arrange the ingredients on the plate, then pour or drizzle the dressing over the top.

Garnishing your salad before serving will also enhance its visual appeal. Garnishes can vary from a single sprig of a herb to chopped herbs sprinkled over the salad, to a single extra ingredient from the salad, such as a shrimp in its shell or a scallion tassel.

Finally, cooking and eating should be fun! Enjoy preparing and eating the salads on the following pages, but do be flexible too and experiment with the almost infinite variety of beautiful and delicious ingredients available.

**RIGHT:** This Three-Melon Salad (see page 66) shows how simple melon balls can look stunning. Decorative shapes for fruits and vegetables can be cut using a citrus stripper, zester or peeler.

# ALL-AMERICAN SALADS

This chapter includes classic favorites, such as the Waldorf Salad and the Caesar Salad, the stylish salad invented in 1924 by Caesar Cardini, which is usually finished with a flourish at your table in good restaurants. Also featured are salads that reflect the ethnic diversity of America, such as German Hot Potato Salad, and the range of ingredients available, such as the Lobster & Avocado Salad.

## CLASSIC COLESLAW

8 ounces white cabbage
6 ounces carrots
3 stalks celery
2 small shallots, peeled
3 tablespoons snipped fresh chives

### DRESSING

6 tablespoons mayonnaise
3 tablespoons sour cream
1 tablespoon white wine vinegar
1 tablespoon water
½ teaspoon sugar
Salt and ground black pepper

Shred the cabbage finely. Peel the carrots and grate them coarsely. Slice the celery thinly and chop the shallots very finely. Place in a large bowl and add the snipped chives.

Place the dressing ingredients in a separate bowl and whisk well to combine. Pour the dressing over the vegetables and toss to coat. Refrigerate for at least 1 hour before serving to let the flavors develop.

SERVES 6

## FRUIT & NUT SLAW

4 ounces red cabbage
4 ounces white cabbage
4 scallions
1 carrot
2 red apples
1 cup halved Brazil nuts
4 tablespoons raisins
1 tablespoon chopped fresh parsley, to garnish

### DRESSING

⅔ cup mayonnaise
2 tablespoons water
½ teaspoon sugar
2 tablespoons lemon juice
Salt and ground black pepper

Shred the two cabbages finely. Slice the scallions thinly, and peel and shred the carrot. Quarter and core the apples and slice them thinly. Place the prepared vegetables and fruit in a bowl with the nuts and raisins.

Place all the dressing ingredients in a bowl and whisk well to combine. Pour the dressing over the prepared ingredients in the bowl and toss well to combine. Refrigerate for 1 hour to let the flavors develop. Serve garnished with chopped parsley.

SERVES 6

**TOP:** Fruit & Nut Slaw
**BOTTOM:** Classic Coleslaw

# SHRIMP & COTTAGE CHEESE SALAD IN CAPSICUM CUPS

1½ cups cottage cheese
2 tablespoons chopped fresh dill
6 ounces cooked, peeled shrimp
¾ cup seedless green grapes
1 large shallot
Salt and ground black pepper
1 medium red bell pepper
1 medium green bell pepper
4 ounces crisp lettuce leaves
½ quantity Classic French Dressing (see page 74)
4 small cooked shrimp in the shell and dill sprigs,
to garnish

Place the cottage cheese, dill and shrimp in a mixing bowl. Wash and halve the grapes and chop the shallot finely. Add the grapes and shallot to the bowl and season the mixture well. Mix gently to combine.

Halve the bell peppers lengthwise, keeping the stalks intact. Remove the cores and seeds and discard. Toss the washed and dried lettuce leaves in the dressing and divide between four plates. Spoon one-quarter of the cottage cheese and shrimp mixture into each pepper half. Place a filled pepper on each plate with the lettuce. Garnish each serving with a whole shrimp and dill sprigs, and serve at once.        SERVES 4

# COBB SALAD

*This salad has been made with blue Brie instead of Roquefort for a unique variation on an old favorite. You may, of course, prefer to substitute Roquefort or another blue cheese for the Brie in the recipe.*

4 hard-boiled eggs
8 ounces blue Brie cheese
8 ounces cooked, skinless, boneless chicken breast
12 slices bacon
6 tomatoes
12 stuffed green olives
12 pitted black olives
5 cups shredded iceberg lettuce
Blue Cheese Dressing, made with blue Brie
(see page 76)

Shell and slice the hard-boiled eggs. Slice the blue Brie into long thin slices. Cut the chicken into thin strips.

Cook the bacon under a preheated hot broiler for about 10 minutes, turning halfway through, until it is crispy. Let cool, then snip into bite-size pieces.

Cut the tomatoes into quarters, remove the seeds, and chop the flesh roughly. Halve the olives.

Divide the shredded lettuce between four plates. Arrange the prepared ingredients in rows on top of the lettuce. Spoon one-quarter of the dressing onto each salad and serve immediately.

SERVES 4 AS A MAIN COURSE

**RIGHT:** Shrimp & Cottage Cheese Salad
in Capsicum Cups

## CAESAR SALAD

2 large slices, day-old white bread
½ cup olive oil
2 cloves garlic, crushed
I Romaine lettuce
8 anchovy fillets
½ cup grated Parmesan cheese

### DRESSING
I large egg
I clove garlic, crushed
I teaspoon Dijon mustard
⅔ cup extra virgin olive oil
2 tablespoons white wine vinegar
Salt and ground black pepper

Prepare the croutons. Remove crusts from the bread and discard. Cut the bread into small cubes. Heat half the oil and garlic in a skillet, add half the cubed bread, and fry over a medium heat for 2-3 minutes until golden. Remove with a slotted spoon and drain on paper towels. Repeat with the remaining oil, garlic and bread.

Wash and dry the Romaine lettuce, and tear into 2-inch pieces. Place in a large serving bowl. Drain and rinse the anchovies, and snip finely. Add to the lettuce with half the Parmesan.

Make the dressing. Place the egg in a food processor with the garlic and mustard. With the motor running, pour the oil on the egg in a thin steady stream, until a thick emulsion is produced. Add the vinegar, salt and pepper, and blend again briefly.

To serve, pour the dressing over the salad and toss gently. Sprinkle over the remaining Parmesan and scatter over the croutons. Serve at once. SERVES 4

*Variation: Chopped crisply-cooked bacon can be added to this salad for a tasty alternative.*

## WESTERN SALAD

2 large slices, day-old white bread
Corn oil for deep-frying
I Romaine lettuce
I ounce arugula leaves
1½ cups cubed blue cheese
¼ cup grated Parmesan cheese
2 tablespoons snipped fresh chives

### DRESSING
I egg
2 cloves garlic, crushed
⅔ cup corn oil
2 tablespoons lemon juice
Salt and ground black pepper

Prepare the croutons. Remove crusts from the bread and discard. Cut the bread into small cubes. Heat the oil for deep-frying. When it is hot enough (a cube of bread dropped into the oil sizzles at the surface), fry the bread in batches for about 30 seconds, until golden. Remove with a slotted spoon and drain on paper towels.

Make the dressing. Cook the egg in boiling water for 2 minutes to lightly soft-boil it. Then spoon the soft egg into a food processor and add the garlic. With the motor running, pour the oil onto the egg in a steady stream to produce a creamy dressing. Add the lemon juice and seasoning, and blend again briefly.

Wash and dry the Romaine lettuce, and tear into bite-size pieces. Place in a salad bowl with the washed arugula. Add the cubed blue cheese and Parmesan.

To serve, pour the dressing over and toss gently. Scatter the croutons and snipped chives on top, and serve at once. SERVES 4

**TOP:** Caesar Salad
**BOTTOM:** Western Salad

# WALDORF SALAD

9 ounces Florence fennel
2 tablespoons lemon juice
2 red apples
4 ounces red lettuce leaves, such as oak leaf
½ cup toasted walnut pieces
¼ cup raisins
Fennel fronds, to garnish

### DRESSING

6 tablespoons mayonnaise
2 tablespoons walnut oil
2 tablespoons lemon juice
Salt and ground black pepper

Reserve the fennel fronds and slice the Florence fennel bulb thinly. Place in a bowl with the lemon juice, tossing gently to coat. Quarter and core the apples, and slice them. Add the apples to the bowl with the fennel, and toss to coat with lemon juice.

Wash and dry the lettuce. Line a shallow serving dish with the leaves. Place the dressing ingredients in a bowl and whisk well to combine.

Just before serving, drain the fennel and apple and add to the bowl of dressing, along with the walnuts and raisins. Toss to combine and spoon the salad onto the bed of lettuce. Garnish with the fennel fronds, and serve at once.      SERVES 4-6

# SWEDISH SALAD

6 ounces celery
8 ounces cooked red beets
2 red apples
½ cup toasted walnut halves
4 ounces radicchio leaves

### DRESSING

6 tablespoons mayonnaise
2 tablespoons lemon juice
2 tablespoons sour cream
Salt and ground black pepper

Slice the celery thinly on the diagonal. Cut the red beets into wedges. Peel and core the apples, and slice them. Place the celery, beets and apple in a large bowl. Reserve a few walnuts for garnish and add the rest to the bowl.

Place the dressing ingredients in a bowl and whisk to combine. Pour the dressing over the prepared ingredients. Toss well to mix and set aside.

Wash and dry the radicchio leaves, and tear them in half. Line a salad bowl with the leaves and spoon the tossed salad into the center. Garnish with the reserved walnuts, and serve at once.      SERVES 4-6

**TOP:** Swedish Salad
**BOTTOM:** Waldorf Salad

# FLORIDA SHRIMP SALAD

20 cooked jumbo shrimp in the shell
4 pink grapefruit
1-pound piece honeydew melon
8 ounces iceberg lettuce
4 teaspoons fresh chervil leaves

### DRESSING
6 tablespoons grapeseed oil
6 tablespoons mayonnaise
2 tablespoons champagne vinegar
3 tablespoons water
1 shallot, finely chopped
1 tablespoon crushed dried pink peppercorns
Salt and ground black pepper

Peel 12 of the shrimp and halve each shrimp lengthwise. Keep 8 shrimp whole, for garnishing. Peel the grapefruit and cut in between the membranes to produce sections.

Using a melon baller, scoop balls from the melon flesh. Wash and dry the lettuce, and tear the leaves into bite-size pieces.

Place the ingredients for the dressing in a bowl and whisk together to combine.

To assemble the salads, divide the lettuce between four plates. Arrange the prepared shrimp, grapefruit sections and melon balls on the plates, spoon the dressing over the four salads, and scatter the chervil leaves on top. Garnish each plate with 2 whole shrimp, and serve at once. SERVES 4 AS A MAIN COURSE

# CHEF'S SALAD

2 tablespoons vegetable oil
12 ounces raw, skinless, boneless pieces turkey breast
Salt and ground black pepper
4 thick slices smoked ham
8 ounces Gruyère or Emmentaler cheese
4 small tomatoes
4 hard-boiled eggs
1 small head iceberg lettuce
Thousand Island Dressing (see page 76)
Parsley sprigs, to garnish

Heat the oil in a heavy-bottomed skillet. Season the pieces of turkey breast with salt and pepper, and add to the pan. Cook over a high heat for 10 minutes, turning occasionally, until the turkey is golden on the outside and cooked through. Remove from the skillet and set aside to cool.

Slice the ham into long strips. Using a swivel vegetable peeler, slice the cheese very thinly. Cut the tomatoes into wedges and shell and slice the eggs. Shred the lettuce finely. When the turkey has cooled, slice it into neat pieces.

Assemble the salads. Divide the shredded lettuce between four large plates. Arrange equal amounts of turkey, ham, cheese, tomato and egg on each plate. Spoon a little dressing into the center of each salad and garnish with parsley. Serve at once, passing extra dressing separately. SERVES 4 AS A MAIN COURSE

**RIGHT:** Florida Shrimp Salad

## SWEET POTATO SALAD

2 pounds sweet potatoes
8 ounces carrots
I green bell pepper
4 tablespoons torn cilantro leaves
Salt and ground black pepper

### BUTTERMILK HERB DRESSING
6 tablespoons buttermilk
4 tablespoons mayonnaise
I tablespoon finely chopped fresh cilantro
I tablespoon snipped fresh chives
Salt and ground black pepper

Preheat the oven to 350°F. Bake the sweet potatoes for about 40 minutes, until tender. Remove from the oven and set aside to cool. When cool, peel off the skin and cut flesh into large dice.

Peel the carrots and slice them thickly. Blanch in boiling, salted water for 2-3 minutes, then drain and refresh in cold water. Halve the bell pepper, remove the core and seeds, and dice the flesh.

Place the dressing ingredients in a bowl and mix to combine. Place the sweet potato, carrot, pepper and torn cilantro in a bowl, season well, and pour the dressing over the top. Toss gently to combine. Refrigerate the salad for 2 hours before serving to let the flavors develop. SERVES 4-6

## GERMAN HOT POTATO SALAD

I pound boiling potatoes
2 tablespoons vegetable oil
8 slices bacon, diced
I small red onion
4 teaspoons chopped fresh sage

### DRESSING
6 tablespoons mayonnaise
2 tablespoons milk
2 tablespoons sour cream
2 teaspoons coarse-grain mustard
Salt and ground black pepper

Place all the dressing ingredients in a bowl and mix well to combine. Set aside.

Peel the potatoes and cut into chunks. Cook the potatoes in boiling, salted water for about 8 minutes, until tender. Drain and keep warm.

While the potatoes are cooking, heat the oil in a skillet and fry the bacon for 8-9 minutes until crisp. Keep warm.

Dice the onion finely. Place the onion, hot potatoes and bacon in a mixing bowl with the sage. Pour the dressing over, toss well, and serve the salad warm.
SERVES 4

**TOP:** German Hot Potato Salad
**BOTTOM:** Sweet Potato Salad

# CHICKEN, GRAPE & HAZELNUT SALAD

1 pound cooked chicken breasts
1½ cups black grapes
4 tablespoons toasted, skinless hazelnuts
Salt and ground black pepper
8 ounces watercress
Fresh tarragon leaves, to garnish

### DRESSING
2 scallions
6 tablespoons mayonnaise
4 tablespoons cream cheese
6 tablespoons water
Salt and ground black pepper

Remove the skin from the cooked chicken and discard. Cut the meat into bite-size chunks and place in a large mixing bowl.

Wash the grapes, halve them, and remove the seeds. Add the grapes to the chicken, along with the toasted hazelnuts. Season with salt and pepper, and mix gently to combine.

Prepare the dressing. Chop the scallions finely and place in a bowl. Add the remaining dressing ingredients and mix well. Pour the creamy dressing over the chicken and toss gently to coat.

Discard the tough stalks from the watercress. Wash and dry the watercress.

To serve, arrange a bed of watercress on a platter and spoon the chicken mixture into the center. Garnish with tarragon, and serve at once.     SERVES 4

# ASPARAGUS & EGG SALAD

1 pound fresh asparagus stalks
4 hard-boiled eggs
8 slices pastrami

### BUTTERMILK DRESSING
4 tablespoons buttermilk
4 tablespoons olive oil
2 tablespoons white wine vinegar
2 teaspoons coarse-grain mustard
Salt and ground black pepper

Cut the tough ends off the asparagus stalks and, using a vegetable peeler, peel the green skin from the asparagus stalks, stopping just below the tips. Blanch the asparagus in boiling, salted water for 2-3 minutes, until just cooked. Drain and refresh in cold water.

Shell the eggs and slice each egg into 4-6 wedges. Place the ingredients for the Buttermilk Dressing in a bowl and whisk to combine.

To serve, arrange the asparagus, egg wedges and pastrami on four serving plates. Drizzle some dressing over each portion, and serve at once.     SERVES 4

**RIGHT:** Chicken, Grape & Hazelnut Salad

# LOBSTER & AVOCADO SALAD

2 small, boiled lobsters
8 asparagus stalks, preferably white
1 large, ripe avocado
4 teaspoons lemon juice
4 ounces mixed lettuce leaves
Tarragon sprigs, to garnish

### DRESSING

2 tablespoons olive oil
4 tablespoons sunflower oil
2 tablespoons tarragon vinegar
2 teaspoons finely chopped shallot
4 teaspoons chopped fresh tarragon
2 teaspoons Dijon mustard
1 teaspoon sugar
Salt and ground black pepper

Prepare the lobsters. Twist off the claws and crack them. Either leave the claws ready for eating or remove the flesh. For each lobster, gently separate the tail from the head and body. With sharp scissors, cut down the length of the underside of the tail. Bend apart so the meat becomes free, and remove the vein. Remove the flesh and slice into thick discs.

Cut the tough ends from the asparagus and slice each stalk in half lengthwise. Blanch in boiling, salted water for 2 minutes. Drain and refresh under cold water. Peel the avocado, halve and slice the flesh thickly; then place in a bowl with the lemon juice.

Wash and dry the lettuce. Place the dressing ingredients in a bowl and whisk to combine.

To assemble, toss the lettuce with half the dressing and divide between two plates. Arrange the lobster, asparagus and avocado on each bed of lettuce. Spoon the remaining dressing over the salads, garnish with tarragon, and serve at once.

SERVES 2 AS A MAIN COURSE

# CRAB LOUIS SALAD

3 cups fresh crabmeat
1 onion
4 ounces celery
12 stuffed olives
Salt and ground black pepper
Pinch of cayenne pepper
4 ounces iceberg lettuce
Celery leaves, to garnish

### DRESSING

4 tablespoons mayonnaise
4 tablespoons light cream, very lightly whipped
4 tablespoons chili sauce
1 small green chili, seeded and chopped
4 tablespoons fresh chervil leaves
Salt and ground black pepper

Place all the dressing ingredients in a bowl and mix well to combine. Refrigerate while preparing the salad to let the flavors develop.

Flake the crabmeat and place in a mixing bowl. Peel the onion and grate coarsely. Wash the celery and slice thinly on the diagonal. Halve the olives. Add the ingredients to the crabmeat and season with salt, pepper and cayenne pepper. Add the dressing and toss well.

Wash and dry the lettuce. Divide the lettuce between four plates and spoon one-quarter of the crab salad onto each plate. Garnish with celery leaves, and serve at once. SERVES 4

**TOP:** Crab Louis Salad
**BOTTOM:** Lobster & Avocado Salad

## WILD RICE SALAD WITH SCALLOPS

1 cup mixed long-grain and wild rice
2 scallions
2 large carrots
½ red bell pepper
½ orange bell pepper
2 tablespoons pumpkin seeds
1 pound large scallops, with roes
3 tablespoons vegetable oil

### DRESSING
Grated zest of 1 lime
4 tablespoons lime juice
6 tablespoons sunflower oil
1 large clove garlic, crushed
4 teaspoons chopped fresh flat-leaf parsley
Pinch of sugar
Salt and ground black pepper

Cook the rice in boiling, salted water according to the instructions on the package. Drain and refresh in cold water. Set aside.

Slice the scallions into long, thin strips. Peel the carrots and, using a vegetable peeler, peel the carrots into long ribbons. Blanch the carrot ribbons in boiling, salted water for about 1 minute. Drain and refresh in cold water.

Remove the cores from the peppers and dice the flesh finely. Toast the pumpkin seeds under a hot broiler for 2 minutes, until pale golden. Remove the seeds and let cool.

Separate the scallop roes from the whites. Cut each scallop white into quarters and halve the roes. Heat half the oil in a skillet and sauté the whites, stirring frequently, for about 3 minutes. Remove the scallops from the skillet. Add the remaining oil to the skillet and sauté the roes for 3 minutes. Remove the roes from the skillet.

Place the ingredients for the dressing in a screw-topped jar and shake well to mix. Pour half the dressing over the rice and toss gently to coat. Place the rice in a serving dish.

Mix together the remaining ingredients, except the pumpkin seeds, and pour the remaining dressing over the top. Toss gently and spoon over the rice. Scatter the pumpkin seeds on top and serve at once.

SERVES 4-6

## BLACK-EYED SUSAN SALAD

4 grapefruit
4 dates
⅓ cup pecans
6 ounces mixed lettuce leaves, to include arugula, Romaine and corn salad
Classic French Dressing (see page 74)

Using a sharp knife, peel the skin and white pith from the grapefruit and cut between the membranes to produce sections.

Remove the pits from the dates and slice the flesh into long sections. Cut the pecans lengthwise into quarters. Wash and dry the lettuce, and tear large leaves into bite-size pieces.

To serve, toss the lettuce with half the dressing and divide between four plates. Arrange the grapefruit in a spoke-like pattern over the lettuce, and arrange the dates and pecans in the center. Spoon the remaining dressing over the salads, and serve at once.

SERVES 4

**TOP:** Wild Rice Salad with Scallops
**BOTTOM:** Black-eyed Susan Salad

# EUROPEAN SALADS

The surprisingly diverse flavors and ingredients of this small continent feature in the recipes in this chapter. Along with Caponata from Sicily, with its colorful variety of vegetables, and the French Salade Niçoise, with its Mediterranean taste, are the German Kartoffelsalat and the Norwegian Herring & Dill Salad, with their subtler, northern flavors.

## GREEK SALAD

12 ounces feta cheese
4 plum tomatoes
I small cucumber
I small purple onion
16 oil-cured Greek olives
Oregano sprigs, to garnish

### HERB DRESSING
6 tablespoons extra virgin olive oil, preferably Greek
2 tablespoons white wine vinegar
3 tablespoons chopped fresh oregano
I large clove garlic, crushed
Pinch of sugar
Salt and ground black pepper

Place all the dressing ingredients in a screw-topped jar and shake well to combine. Chill until required.

Cube the feta cheese and cut the tomatoes into wedges. Place in a large salad bowl.

Halve the cucumber and dice. Peel and thinly slice the onion. Add the cucumber and onion to the salad with the olives. Pour the dressing over the top and toss well. Serve at once.          SERVES 4

## TOMATO SALAD WITH HALLOUMI & ARUGULA

8 small, ripe plum tomatoes
4 ounces halloumi cheese
2 scallions
5 ounces arugula leaves
12 black olives

### DRESSING
6 tablespoons extra virgin olive oil
2 tablespoons red wine vinegar
2 tablespoons chopped fresh oregano
Salt and ground black pepper
Pinch of sugar

Wash the tomatoes and slice thickly. Cut the halloumi cheese into thin strips. Shred the scallions into long, thin strips.

Wash and dry the arugula and tear any large leaves into bite-size pieces; then line a serving plate with the leaves. Arrange the tomatoes and cheese on the bed of arugula, and scatter the scallions and olives over the top.

Place the dressing ingredients in a screw-topped jar and shake well to combine. Spoon the dressing over the prepared salad, and serve at once.    SERVES 4-6

**TOP:** Greek Salad
**BOTTOM:** Tomato Salad with Halloumi & Arugula

# FRENCH LEAF SALAD WITH GARLIC CROUTONS

6 ounces curly endive

### GARLIC CROUTONS
4 cloves garlic, crushed
6 tablespoons extra virgin olive oil
Salt and ground black pepper
2 slices crustless white bread

### ROQUEFORT DRESSING
3 tablespoons corn oil
3 tablespoons mayonnaise
2 tablespoons white wine vinegar
2 tablespoons water
½ teaspoon Dijon mustard
Few drops Worcestershire sauce
Salt and ground black pepper
4 ounces Roquefort cheese

Prepare the croutons. Preheat the oven to 350°F. Place the garlic, oil and seasoning in a large bowl and mix well. Cut the bread into ½-inch cubes and add to the bowl. Toss well to coat. Transfer the bread to a baking sheet and bake on the top shelf of the oven for about 15 minutes, until golden. Remove and set aside.

Place all the dressing ingredients, except the cheese, in a bowl and whisk to combine. Mash the cheese with a fork and add it, a little at a time, to the dressing, whisking well between each addition.

Wash and dry the curly endive and tear into bite-size pieces. Place in a bowl with half the croutons, pour the dressing over, and toss until evenly coated with dressing. Serve the salad at once with the remaining croutons scattered over the top.          SERVES 4

# SALADE NICOISE

2 cups canned tuna in oil, drained and flaked
1 cup thin green beans
⅔ cup baby fava beans, peeled
6 anchovy fillets
1 small cucumber
4 tomatoes
20 black olives
3 hard-boiled eggs, shelled
Belgian endive leaves, to serve

### DRESSING
6 tablespoons French olive oil
2 tablespoons white wine vinegar
1 clove garlic, crushed
1 teaspoon Dijon mustard
3 tablespoons chopped flat-leaf parsley
Salt and ground black pepper

Place the dressing ingredients in a screw-topped jar and shake well to combine. Set aside.

Place the flaked tuna in a mixing bowl. Halve the green beans and blanch them in boiling, salted water with the fava beans for 3 minutes, until just tender. Drain and refresh in cold water.

Cut the anchovy fillets into small pieces and slice the cucumber into batons. Cut the tomatoes into wedges. Add beans, anchovy, cucumber and tomato to the tuna, along with the olives. Pour the dressing over, and toss the salad gently.

Wash and dry the endive and line a serving dish with the leaves. Spoon the prepared salad into the center. Cut each egg into quarters and add to the salad. Serve at once.          SERVES 4

**TOP:** French Leaf Salad
**BOTTOM:** Salade Niçoise

# WARM CHICKEN LIVER, SUN-DRIED TOMATO & PASTA SALAD

8 ounces dried pasta shapes
4 tablespoons olive oil
3 shallots, sliced
2 cloves garlic, crushed
1 pound chicken livers, trimmed
Salt and ground black pepper
8 halves sun-dried tomatoes in oil, drained and sliced
1½ cups washed and torn curly endive

## DRESSING

4 tablespoons oil from sun-dried tomatoes
4 tablespoons olive oil
4 tablespoons balsamic vinegar
4 tablespoons chopped fresh parsley
2 teaspoons Dijon mustard
Salt and ground black pepper

Place all the dressing ingredients in a screw-topped jar and shake well.

Cook the pasta in plenty of boiling, salted water for about 10 minutes or until "al dente." Drain the pasta and immediately toss it with the prepared dressing while still warm. Set aside.

Heat the oil in a large skillet and sauté the shallots and garlic for 1 minute, until softened. Add the chicken livers, season well, and sauté for a further 4-5 minutes, until browned on the outside and just cooked in the center. Transfer the chicken livers to the bowl of pasta. Add the sun-dried tomatoes and toss well to combine. Serve the warm salad immediately, on a bed of curly endive. SERVES 6

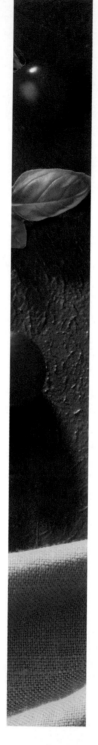

# SMOKED DUCK & PESTO PASTA SALAD

4 ounces dried pasta shapes
6 ounces cooked, smoked duck breast
12 cherry tomatoes
4 tablespoons toasted pine nuts
6 ounces mixed salad leaves
Basil sprigs, to garnish

## PESTO DRESSING

4 tablespoons pesto sauce
6 tablespoons vegetable oil
2 tablespoons red wine vinegar
Salt and ground black pepper

Place all the dressing ingredients in a bowl and whisk to combine.

Cook the pasta in plenty of boiling, salted water for 8-10 minutes or until "al dente." Drain the pasta and immediately toss it with the dressing. Set aside.

Slice the duck into thin strips and halve the cherry tomatoes. Add to the bowl of pasta, along with the pine nuts. Toss well.

Wash the lettuce leaves and tear large leaves in half. Line a serving bowl with the lettuce and spoon the pasta salad into the center. Garnish with basil, and serve at once. SERVES 4

**RIGHT:** Smoked Duck & Pesto Pasta Salad

# AVOCADO, MOZZARELLA & BAKED TOMATO SALAD

*The baked tomatoes in this salad take a long time to cook and, for convenience, can be prepared the day before and stored in an airtight container in the refrigerator until required.*

5 ounces mini mozzarella cheeses
2 ripe avocados
1 tablespoon lemon juice
Basil leaves, to garnish

### BAKED TOMATOES

6 small, ripe plum tomatoes
Olive oil to drizzle
A little superfine sugar
Sea salt and ground black pepper

### DRESSING

½ cup extra virgin olive oil
2 tablespoons balsamic vinegar
4 tablespoons torn basil leaves
Salt and ground black pepper

Prepare the baked tomatoes. Preheat the oven to 200°F. Blanch the tomatoes for 20 seconds in boiling, salted water to loosen their skins. When cooled, peel off the skin, halve, and scoop out the seeds. Place cut-side down on a greased baking sheet. Drizzle each tomato with a little olive oil and sprinkle with a little sugar, salt and pepper. Bake for 1 hour. Turn over, drizzle with a little more oil, and bake for a further hour. Remove and let cool.

Slice the mini mozzarella into thick slices. Peel and pit the avocados, and slice the flesh. Sprinkle the avocados with lemon juice.

Mix together the dressing ingredients. To serve, arrange the tomatoes, cheese and avocado on four plates. Spoon dressing over each salad, garnish with basil, and serve at once. SERVES 4

# ARUGULA, BACON & AVOCADO SALAD

12 slices bacon
2 small avocados
1 tablespoon lemon juice
6 ounces arugula leaves
6 tablespoons finely grated Parmesan cheese
Ground black pepper
Italian Balsamic Dressing (see page 74)

Place the bacon slices under a preheated broiler and broil for about 8 minutes, turning halfway through cooking, until crisp and golden. Remove and drain on paper towels. When cool, snip the bacon into bite-size pieces with kitchen scissors.

Peel and pit the avocado, and cut the flesh into chunks. Place in a bowl with the lemon juice. Wash and dry the arugula leaves, and place in a salad bowl. Add the bacon, avocado and 4 tablespoons of the Parmesan. Add some black pepper and pour the prepared dressing over. Toss the salad gently, and serve with the remaining Parmesan sprinkled over the top.

SERVES 4

**TOP:** Avocado, Mozzarella
& Baked Tomato Salad
**BOTTOM:** Arugula, Bacon & Avocado Salad

## CAPONATA

*This salad is best made a day ahead and stored in the refrigerator to let the flavors develop.*

6 tablespoons extra virgin olive oil
I red onion, sliced into rings
2 cloves garlic, sliced into slivers
I large eggplant
2 ripe beefsteak tomatoes
2 zucchini
2 yellow bell peppers
2 tablespoons sun-dried tomato paste
Salt and ground black pepper
2 tablespoons red wine vinegar
2 tablespoons chopped fresh flat-leaf parsley
I tablespoon chopped fresh thyme
16 small black olives
8 anchovy fillets
2 crisp lettuce hearts, washed and separated
into leaves
Flat-leaf parsley sprig, to garnish

Preheat the oven to 350°F. Heat half the oil in a large, heavy-bottomed, flameproof saucepan. Add the onion and sauté for 2 minutes. Stir in the garlic and sauté for a further minute. Set aside.

Cut the eggplant into ½-inch cubes. Peel and seed the tomatoes, and cut into large dice. Slice the zucchini. Cut the bell peppers into ½-inch cubes. Add the vegetables to the pan.

Stir the sun-dried tomato paste into the pan and season the vegetables well. Cook over a low heat for 5 minutes, then cover the pan and transfer to the oven. Bake for 40 minutes.

Place the remaining olive oil in a screw-topped jar with the vinegar, parsley, thyme and seasoning. Shake well to combine. Cut each anchovy fillet into four.

Stir the dressing, anchovies and olives into the warm vegetables. Let cool.

Just before serving, line a dish with the lettuce leaves. Using a slotted spoon, spoon the caponata onto the lettuce. Serve garnished with parsley sprigs.

SERVES 4

## ORANGE & PURPLE ONION SALAD

6 large oranges
I large purple onion
12 black olives (optional)

**POPPYSEED DRESSING**
6 tablespoons extra virgin olive oil
2 tablespoons fresh orange juice
I tablespoon white wine vinegar
1½ teaspoons clear honey
2 teaspoons poppyseeds
Salt and ground black pepper

Peel the oranges using a small sharp knife, taking care to remove all the white pith. Slice the oranges thickly and arrange them in overlapping circles on a shallow serving plate.

Slice the purple onion into thin rings. Arrange the onion on top of the oranges and scatter the black olives over the top, if desired.

Place the dressing ingredients in a screw-topped jar and shake well to combine. Spoon the dressing over the salad, and serve at once. SERVES 4-6

**TOP:** Caponata
**BOTTOM:** Orange & Purple Onion Salad

## GREEN LENTIL SALAD

1 cup Puy lentils, soaked for 1 hour
1 orange bell pepper
1 red bell pepper
3 scallions
4 ounces escarole leaves
Oregano sprigs, to garnish

### DRESSING

4 tablespoons plain yogurt
2 tablespoons olive oil
3 tablespoons chopped fresh parsley
3 tablespoons chopped fresh oregano
1 large clove garlic, crushed
¼ teaspoon paprika
Salt and ground black pepper

Place all the dressing ingredients in a bowl and whisk to combine. Set aside.

Drain the soaked lentils and place in a saucepan of fresh water with a little salt. Boil the lentils gently for about 20 minutes or until tender, then drain. While still warm, toss the lentils with the dressing to let the flavors absorb. Set aside.

Halve the bell peppers and remove the cores and seeds. Broil under a preheated broiler for about 10 minutes, until the skins are charred. Remove and cover the peppers with damp paper towels to make them easier to peel. When cool, peel off the skins and slice the flesh into thin strips. Chop the scallions finely and add to the lentils, along with the peppers. Toss well. Wash and dry the lettuce leaves, and serve the salad on a bed of escarole, garnished with oregano sprigs.

SERVES 6

## TURKISH SALAD

*Labna balls are strained yogurt balls preserved in oil. Herbs are sometimes added to the oil. They are available in jars from good continental delicatessens.*

2 zucchini
½ onion
8 labna balls in oil, drained
6 artichoke hearts in oil, drained
1 Romaine lettuce
4 tablespoons finely diced red bell pepper

### DRESSING

2 tablespoons oil from the jar of labna balls
2 tablespoons extra virgin olive oil
2 tablespoons lemon juice
½ teaspoon ground cumin
¼ teaspoon chili powder
Salt and ground black pepper
Pinch of sugar

Place all the dressing ingredients in a small saucepan. Whisk to combine and heat the dressing very gently to warm it.

Using a vegetable peeler, peel long ribbons of zucchini. Slice the onion very thinly. Place the zucchini ribbons and sliced onions in a bowl, pour over the warm dressing, and toss gently to combine. Set aside.

Halve the labna balls and the artichokes. Wash and dry the lettuce, and tear the leaves into bite-size pieces. Divide the lettuce between four plates. Add the labna balls and artichoke hearts to the zucchini and onions, and toss gently to coat with the dressing. Divide the mixture between the plates. Sprinkle one-quarter of the diced red bell pepper over each salad, and serve at once.

SERVES 4

**RIGHT:** Turkish Salad

## GREEK PEACH & GRILLED GREEN PEPPER SALAD

4 green bell peppers
2 large, ripe peaches
6 ounces feta cheese
12 kalamata olives

### CUMIN DRESSING

2 teaspoons cumin seeds
½ cup olive oil
3 tablespoons white wine vinegar
Salt and ground black pepper
Pinch of sugar

Halve the bell peppers lengthwise, and remove the cores and seeds. Place them, cut-side down, on a baking sheet and broil under a preheated hot broiler for 8-10 minutes, or until the skins are charred. Remove and cover the peppers with damp paper towels to make them easier to peel. When cool, peel off the charred skins and slice the flesh into thick strips.

Halve and pit the peaches, and slice the flesh thickly. Cut the feta into small cubes. Place the peppers, peaches, feta and olives in a mixing bowl.

Make the dressing. Dry-fry the cumin seeds in a skillet for about 1 minute, until they begin to pop and their aroma is released. Transfer to a bowl with the remaining dressing ingredients and mix well.

Pour the dressing over the salad ingredients and toss gently. Refrigerate for 1 hour before serving.

SERVES 4

## SPICED RICE SALAD

½ cup brown long-grain rice
½ cup white long-grain rice
¼ cup fresh dates
½ cup dried apricots
⅓ cup shelled pistachio nuts
4 tablespoons snipped fresh chives
Cilantro sprigs, to garnish

### DRESSING

5 tablespoons pistachio or corn oil
3 tablespoons lime juice
3 tablespoons chopped fresh cilantro
½ teaspoon chili powder
Salt and ground black pepper

Place all the dressing ingredients in a screw-topped jar and shake well to combine.

Cook the two types of rice in separate saucepans of boiling, salted water, following the cooking instructions on the packages. When cooked, drain and mix the warm rice with the dressing. The rice will absorb the flavor of the dressing. Set aside.

Remove the pits from the dates and cut the flesh into long slivers. Cut the apricots into quarters. Add the dates and apricots to the rice, along with the pistachios and chives. Toss well. Serve the salad at room temperature, garnished with cilantro sprigs.

SERVES 4

**TOP:** Spiced Rice Salad
**BOTTOM:** Greek Peach & Grilled
Green Pepper Salad

# NORWEGIAN HERRING & DILL SALAD

1 pound baby new potatoes
4 pickled herrings
2 small shallots
12 Belgian endive leaves, preferably red
1 soft lettuce heart

## DRESSING

6 tablespoons sunflower oil
4 tablespoons chopped fresh dill
3 tablespoons Dijon mustard
3 tablespoons cider vinegar
1½-2 tablespoons superfine sugar
Sea salt and ground black pepper

First prepare the dressing. Place the oil, dill, mustard and vinegar in a bowl. Add 1½ tablespoons of the sugar and season generously. Whisk until well combined. Taste and add the extra sugar and more seasoning, if necessary: the dressing should be thick, sweet and mustardy. Set aside.

Scrub the potatoes. Place in a saucepan of salted water, bring to a boil, then reduce heat and cook on a medium boil for about 12 minutes, or until tender. Drain and refresh in cold water. When the potatoes are cool enough to handle, slice them thickly.

Slice the herrings into 1-inch pieces. Peel and thinly slice the shallots. Place the potatoes, herrings and shallots in a bowl, pour the dressing over, and toss well.

Separate the lettuce heart into leaves. Wash and dry the lettuce and endive leaves. Line a serving bowl with the leaves and spoon the salad into the center. Serve at once.                                    SERVES 4

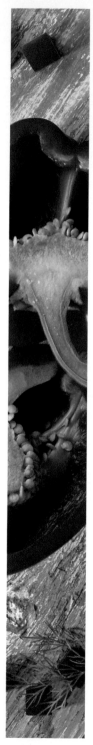

# KARTOFFELSALAT

1 large red bell pepper
2 scallions
1 pound baby new potatoes
8 small, thin German frankfurters

## MUSTARD MAYONNAISE

½ cup mayonnaise
4 teaspoons German mustard
2 tablespoons chopped fresh dill
2 tablespoons milk
Pinch of sugar
Salt and ground black pepper

Place all the mayonnaise ingredients in a bowl and whisk to combine. Set the mayonnaise dressing aside, but do not refrigerate it.

Halve the bell pepper, remove the core and seeds, and dice the flesh. Slice the scallions thinly on the diagonal. Place the prepared peppers and scallions in a serving bowl.

Scrub the potatoes and halve them. Place them in a saucepan of salted water, bring to a boil, then reduce heat and cook on a medium boil for 10-12 minutes until tender. Drain the potatoes and add them to the serving bowl.

While the potatoes are cooking, cook the frankfurters according to the instructions on the package. Drain and slice thickly on the diagonal. Add to the serving bowl.

Pour the dressing over the warm potatoes, frankfurters, and prepared peppers and scallions. Toss to combine, and serve at once while the salad is warm.                                    SERVES 4-6

**RIGHT:** Kartoffelsalat

## BRITISH BEEF SALAD

1¼-pound piece tender, lean beef fillet
Ground black pepper
1 tablespoon vegetable oil
1½ pounds baby new potatoes
1 cup shelled and peeled baby fava beans
12 cherry tomatoes
6 ounces soft lettuce heart leaves
Horseradish Dressing (see page 78)
Curly-leaf parsley sprigs, to garnish

Preheat the oven to 225°F. Cut the beef in half and coat each piece generously with pepper. Heat the oil in a heavy-bottomed skillet and sear the pieces of beef over a high heat, turning so they brown all over, for 6-8 minutes. Transfer the beef to a roasting pan and bake for 1 hour and 10 minutes. This method will produce very tender, medium-rare meat. Let beef cool.

Scrub the potatoes and place in a saucepan of salted water. Bring to a boil, then reduce to a medium heat and simmer for 10-12 minutes, until tender. Drain and refresh in cold water. Slice the cooled potatoes in half.

Cook the beans in boiling, salted water for about 5 minutes, until tender. Drain and refresh in cold water. Halve the cherry tomatoes. Slice the cooled beef into strips and place the meat in a bowl with the potatoes, beans and tomatoes. Pour the dressing over the top and toss well.

Wash the lettuce leaves and divide the lettuce between four plates. Spoon one-quarter of the beef salad onto each plate. Garnish with parsley sprigs, and serve at once. SERVES 4 AS A MAIN COURSE

## WARM GOAT CHEESE SALAD

3 ounces mixed salad leaves, to include oak leaf and baby spinach
½ small ripe pear, cored and sliced
4 slices ciabatta bread
6 ounces goat cheese
1 tablespoon walnut oil

### DRESSING

2 tablespoons walnut oil
1 tablespoon vegetable oil
1 tablespoon white wine vinegar
½ teaspoon Dijon mustard
Pinch of sugar
Salt and ground black pepper

Place the dressing ingredients in a screw-topped jar and shake well to combine. Set aside.

Wash and dry the lettuce, and tear large leaves into bite-size pieces. Place in a bowl with the sliced pears and pour the dressing over the top. Toss gently to coat and divide between two plates.

Place the bread under a preheated hot broiler and toast on one side until lightly golden. Remove and turn the bread over.

Slice the cheese into four pieces and place a piece of cheese on the untoasted side of each bread slice. Drizzle with walnut oil and add some black pepper. Return to the broiler and broil for about 2 minutes, or until cheese begins to melt. Place two slices of bread and cheese on each plate of salad, and serve at once.

SERVES 2

**TOP:** British Beef Salad
**BOTTOM:** Warm Goat Cheese Salad

# EXOTIC & ORIENTAL SALADS

*The recipes in this chapter are inspired by the cuisines of South-east Asia and the Far East, as well as the Caribbean and Mexico. For a delicious and substantial main course, try Salmon Teriyaki Salad or, if you like spicy food, experience the robust flavors of Thai Beef Salad. There are also recipes for the vegetarian, such as Mexican Bean Salad and Tofu & Oriental Mushroom Salad.*

## MEXICAN BEAN SALAD

2 cups canned red kidney beans
2 cups canned black-eyed peas
Heart of 1 Romaine lettuce
2 small avocados

### LIME AND CILANTRO DRESSING
Juice of 1½ limes
Grated zest of ½ lime
6 tablespoons sunolive or light olive oil
3 tablespoons chopped fresh cilantro
1 teaspoon crushed pink and black peppercorns
Sea salt and pinch of sugar

Place all the dressing ingredients in a screw-topped jar and shake well to combine. Chill until required.

Rinse the canned beans well. Separate the Romaine lettuce leaves, and wash and dry them.

Line a flat bowl with the lettuce leaves. Peel, pit and slice the avocados, and mix in a large bowl with the beans and dressing. Spoon the salad onto the bed of lettuce, and serve at once.          SERVES 4-6

## MEXICAN FISH SALAD

8 ounces red snapper fillets
Fish stock for poaching
1 small ripe mango
1 green bell pepper
1 fresh red chili
2 stalks celery
3 ounces crisp lettuce leaves
1 tablespoon cilantro leaves, to garnish

### DRESSING
4 tablespoons mayonnaise
1 tablespoon vegetable oil
1 tablespoon chopped fresh cilantro
1 teaspoon cayenne pepper
½ red chili, seeded and finely chopped
Juice of 1 lime
Hot chili sauce, to taste

Poach the snapper fillets in lightly simmering fish stock for 5-6 minutes, until cooked. Remove, discard the stock, and let cool. When cool, flake the fish.

Cut the mango flesh from the pit and slice thinly. Halve, core and seed the bell pepper, and slice the flesh. Slice the chili into rings. Slice the celery on the diagonal. Wash and dry the lettuce, and tear the leaves into bite-size pieces.

Place the dressing ingredients in a bowl and whisk together until combined. Set aside.

To serve, arrange the lettuce, mango, pepper, chili and celery on two plates. Pour the dressing over the fish and toss lightly to combine. Spoon half the fish onto each bed of salad, garnish with cilantro, and serve at once.          SERVES 2 AS A MAIN COURSE

**TOP:** Mexican Bean Salad
**BOTTOM:** Mexican Fish Salad

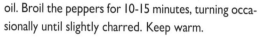

## CAJUN CHICKEN SALAD

4 skinless, boneless chicken breasts
2 tablespoons unsalted butter, melted
2 corn on the cob, each cut into 6 pieces
2 large red bell peppers
2½ cups coarsely shredded iceberg lettuce
Oregano sprigs, to garnish

### SEASONING MIX

1½ teaspoons salt
1 tablespoon paprika
1 teaspoon dried onion flakes
1 teaspoon dried garlic flakes
1 teaspoon dried thyme
1 teaspoon cayenne pepper
½ teaspoon cracked black pepper
½ teaspoon dried oregano

### SPICY DRESSING

6 tablespoons corn oil
2 tablespoons lemon juice
1 shallot, finely chopped
¼ teaspoon cayenne pepper
1 teaspoon Dijon mustard
1 teaspoon chopped fresh thyme
Pinch of sugar
Salt and ground black pepper

Place all the dressing ingredients in a screw-topped jar and shake to combine. Chill until required.

Mix together all the seasoning mix ingredients. Flatten each chicken breast with a meat pounder, between sheets of plastic wrap, until about ½-inch thick. Brush each chicken breast with some melted butter and press one-quarter of the seasoning mix over each breast to coat completely. Set aside.

Cook the corn in boiling, salted water for 20-25 minutes, until tender. Divide each bell pepper in half lengthwise, core and seed, and brush with a little olive oil. Broil the peppers for 10-15 minutes, turning occasionally until slightly charred. Keep warm.

Heat a heavy, cast-iron skillet over a high heat, until the pan is smoking and very hot. Add the chicken and cook for 8-10 minutes, turning occasionally, until the outside is blackened and chicken is cooked.

Toss the iceberg lettuce in the dressing. Cut the red pepper into thick strips. Divide the lettuce between four plates. Slice the chicken breasts and divide between the plates. Place three pieces of corn and some red pepper strips on each plate. Serve at once.

SERVES 4 AS A MAIN COURSE

## TABBOULEH

1½ cups bulghur wheat
2 cups finely chopped flat-leaf parsley
1 cup finely chopped mint leaves
6 scallions, sliced
2 beefsteak tomatoes, skinned, seeded and chopped
1 cup very finely chopped cucumber

### DRESSING

3 cloves garlic, crushed
Juice of 2 lemons
6 tablespoons extra virgin olive oil
Salt and ground black pepper

Place the bulghur wheat in a bowl and just cover with boiling water. Set aside for 30 minutes to let the water absorb. Drain thoroughly, place in a clean linen dish towel, and squeeze to remove excess moisture. Place the bulghur wheat in a large bowl and stir in the remaining ingredients.

Place the dressing ingredients in a screw-topped jar and shake well to combine. Pour over the salad, toss gently, and set aside for 30 minutes before serving to let the flavors develop. SERVES 6

**RIGHT:** Cajun Chicken Salad

# BALINESE DUCK SALAD

2 × 8-ounce duck breasts
Peanut oil for frying
2 ounces Romaine lettuce
2 ounces Chinese bok choy
1 cup washed bean sprouts
4 scallions, sliced on the diagonal
½ cucumber, cut into matchsticks

## MARINADE

4 shallots, chopped
4 cloves garlic, chopped
4 green chilies, seeded and chopped
2-inch piece ginger root, peeled and chopped
½ teaspoon turmeric
2 teaspoons galangal powder
Salt and ground black pepper

## DRESSING

1 tablespoon peanut oil
Juice of 1 lime
3 lime leaves, finely chopped
1 stalk lemon grass, finely chopped
2 teaspoons clear honey
Salt and ground black pepper

Place the marinade ingredients in a blender and process to produce a smooth paste. Slash each duck breast and spread the marinade all over. Refrigerate for at least 1 hour. Place the dressing ingredients in a bowl and whisk to combine. Set aside.

Lightly oil a heavy-bottomed skillet and cook the duck over a high heat for about 6 minutes on each side. Remove from heat. Slice the duck diagonally.

Wash and dry the Romaine and bok choy, and tear the leaves into bite-size pieces. Place in a bowl with the bean sprouts, scallions and cucumber. Pour the dressing over, and toss well. Divide the salad and duck between four plates, and serve at once.  SERVES 4

# CARIBBEAN PORK SALAD

1 pound pork tenderloin, cut into long strips
2 cups cubed pumpkin
2 tablespoons vegetable oil
1 onion, sliced
1 green bell pepper, sliced into rings
1½ cups torn lettuce leaves

## SEASONING MIXTURE

2 teaspoons crushed allspice berries
2 hot Jamaican peppers, seeded and finely chopped
2 teaspoons chopped fresh thyme
2 teaspoons cayenne pepper
2 scallions, finely chopped
2 cloves garlic, crushed
½ teaspoon salt

## DRESSING

4 tablespoons vegetable oil
2 tablespoons white wine vinegar
2 teaspoons chopped fresh thyme
1 teaspoon Dijon mustard
Salt and ground black pepper

Mix the seasoning ingredients together in a bowl. Add the pork strips and toss. Refrigerate for 1 hour.

Boil the cubed pumpkin for about 7 minutes, until tender. Drain and refresh in cold water. Place the dressing ingredients in a screw-topped jar and shake.

Cook the pork in four batches, using one-quarter of the oil for each batch of meat. Cook over a high heat, stirring frequently, for about 2 minutes. Set aside.

Place the sliced onion, green pepper, pumpkin and salad leaves in a bowl. Pour the dressing over, and toss gently. Divide the salad between four plates and top each with one-quarter of the pork. Serve at once.
SERVES 4 AS A MAIN COURSE

**RIGHT:** Caribbean Pork Salad

# ASIAN SQUID & SCALLOP SALAD

Vegetable oil for frying
8 large scallops
12 cleaned baby squid, about 10 ounces in weight
2 scallions
1 star fruit (carambola)
6 ounces Chinese cabbage
4 tablespoons torn cilantro leaves
Cilantro sprigs, to garnish

### LEMON GRASS DRESSING

1 small stalk lemon grass, very finely chopped
3 tablespoons peanut oil
1½ tablespoons soy sauce
1½ tablespoons lemon juice
2 teaspoons sesame oil
1½ teaspoons clear honey
1 large clove garlic, crushed

Place all the dressing ingredients in a screw-topped jar and shake well to combine. Set aside.

Lightly oil and preheat a griddle pan or heavy-bottomed skillet, and cook the scallops over a high heat, for about 5 minute on each side. Remove and set aside. Cook the squid in the skillet for about 1 minute on each side.

Slice the scallions on the diagonal and cut the star fruit into thin slices. Wash the Chinese cabbage and shred coarsely. Toss the cilantro leaves with the cabbage and divide between four plates. Arrange the seafood on the plates with the scallions and star fruit. Spoon dressing over each salad, and serve at once.

SERVES 4 AS A MAIN COURSE

# EXOTIC SHRIMP & PINEAPPLE SALAD

6-ounce piece fresh pineapple
½ small cucumber
2 scallions
3 ounces white cabbage
2 ounces Chinese cabbage
10 cooked jumbo shrimp, peeled but with tails intact
2 cooked jumbo shrimp, in the shell, to garnish
2 wedges fresh pineapple, to garnish
½ teaspoon toasted sesame seeds, to garnish

### DRESSING

1½ tablespoons peanut oil
1½ tablespoons sesame oil
1 tablespoon white wine vinegar
1½ teaspoons soy sauce
1½ teaspoons toasted sesame seeds
1 teaspoon tamarind concentrate
1 teaspoon superfine sugar

Place the dressing ingredients in a screw-topped jar and shake well to combine. Set aside.

Cut the piece of pineapple flesh into slim wedges. Peel and dice the cucumber, and slice the scallions on the diagonal.

Wash the two types of cabbage leaves and shred finely. Toss the shredded cabbage with half the dressing and divide between two plates. Arrange the pineapple, shrimp, cucumber and scallions on top, and spoon the remaining dressing over.

Garnish each salad with a whole shrimp and a wedge of pineapple. Sprinkle the sesame seeds on top, and serve at once.     SERVES 2 AS A MAIN COURSE

**TOP:** Exotic Shrimp & Pineapple Salad
**BOTTOM:** Asian Squid & Scallop Salad

## THAI BEEF SALAD

1-pound piece tender, lean beef fillet
10 ounces Chinese cabbage
1 small cucumber
1½ cups water chestnuts
1 fresh red chili
1 small carrot
1 cup cilantro leaves
2 tablespoons peanut oil

### MARINADE

2 stalks fresh lemon grass, finely chopped
2-inch piece ginger root, peeled and finely chopped
6 lime leaves, finely chopped
2 shallots, finely chopped
4 cloves garlic, crushed
Juice of 2 limes
4 tablespoons brown sugar
4 teaspoons tamarind concentrate
2 teaspoons Thai fish sauce (nam pla)
2 tablespoons chili oil

### DRESSING

2 tablespoons Thai fish sauce (nam pla)
2 tablespoons rice wine vinegar
2 tablespoons peanut oil
4 tablespoons chopped fresh cilantro
Pinch of sugar

Place the marinade ingredients in a large bowl and mix together. Slice the beef into long, thin strips and add to the marinade. Toss well and refrigerate for 1 hour.

Place the dressing ingredients in a screw-topped jar and shake well to combine. Set aside.

Shred the Chinese cabbage and cut the cucumber into long strips. Slice the water chestnuts and cut the chili into rings. Peel the carrot and, using a citrus stripper, make ridges along the length of the carrot; then slice the carrot thinly to produce "flowers."

Place all the prepared vegetables in a large bowl with the cilantro.

Heat a little of the oil in a heavy-bottomed skillet, and fry the beef strips in batches over a high heat, stirring frequently until cooked – about 2 minutes.

To serve, pour the dressing over the raw salad and toss well. Divide between four plates and spoon one-quarter of the beef on each. Serve at once.

SERVES 4 AS A MAIN COURSE

## THAI-STYLE SHRIMP & PAPAYA SALAD

1 ripe papaya
1 pound cooked, peeled shrimp
½ cucumber, cut into matchsticks
¾ cup washed bean sprouts
4 radishes, thinly sliced
2½ cups torn, washed and dried butterhead lettuce
Halved salted peanuts, to garnish

### DRESSING

4 tablespoons peanut oil
2 tablespoons sweet chili sauce
2 teaspoons Thai fish sauce (nam pla)
2 small cloves garlic, crushed
1 small green chili, seeded and finely chopped
Grated zest and juice of 1 lime
½ cup coarsely ground, salted peanuts

Mix the dressing ingredients in a bowl and set aside.

Peel the papaya. Cut the fruit into quarters, remove seeds, and slice the flesh thickly. Place the shrimp, cucumber, bean sprouts, radishes and papaya in a bowl. Pour the dressing over, and toss gently.

Divide the lettuce and shrimp salad between four plates, garnish with peanuts, and serve at once.

SERVES 4 AS A MAIN COURSE

**RIGHT:** Thai Beef Salad

# MUNG BEAN & BASMATI RICE SALAD

½ teaspoon saffron threads
1½ cups boiling water
½ cup mung beans
½ cup basmati rice
2 tablespoons vegetable oil
3 shallots, peeled and diced
4 ounces young spinach leaves
2 large plum tomatoes, peeled, seeded and sliced
½ cup raw cashews
1 teaspoon sea salt

### DRESSING
1 tablespoon vegetable oil
1 tablespoon lime juice
1 tablespoon plain yogurt
1 clove garlic, crushed
Sea salt and pinch of sugar

Place the saffron threads in a bowl with the boiling water and infuse for 30 minutes. Remove 1 tablespoon of saffron liquid and add to the dressing ingredients in a large bowl. Whisk to combine and set aside.

Boil the mung beans for 30-35 minutes, until they have begun to split. Drain and add to the dressing.

Place the infused saffron and its water in a saucepan with a little salt. Bring to a boil, add the rice, and simmer for about 10 minutes until tender. Drain and add to the mung beans.

Heat half the oil in a skillet and sauté the shallots for 2 minutes over a medium-high heat. Add the spinach and sauté for a further minute. Transfer to the bowl of ingredients with the tomatoes.

Heat the remaining oil in a skillet and fry the cashews over a medium-low heat for 5 minutes, turning constantly until golden. Remove, drain on paper towels, and sprinkle with sea salt. Add to the bowl. Toss well, and serve at once.          SERVES 4

# ORIENTAL CRAB SALAD

2 cups snow peas
2 cups baby corn
1 cup bean sprouts
4 cups flaked fresh crabmeat
4 ounces young spinach leaves
Sliced fresh red chili, to garnish

### ROASTED CHILI DRESSING
4 fresh chilies
1 tablespoon grated fresh ginger root
½ cup sunflower oil
4 tablespoons white wine vinegar
2 tablespoons soy sauce
2 teaspoons brown sugar

Prepare the dressing. Place the chilies under a preheated hot broiler and broil, turning once, for 3-4 minutes, until skins are charred. Remove and let cool; then peel off skins, seed, and chop the flesh. Place the chili flesh in a food processor with the remaining dressing ingredients and blend to produce a smooth dressing. Set aside.

Cut the snow peas in half and blanch in boiling, salted water for 30 seconds. Drain and refresh in cold water. Halve the baby corn lengthwise and blanch in boiling, salted water for 1 minute. Drain and refresh in cold water. Wash the bean sprouts. Place the crabmeat, snow peas, corn and bean sprouts in a bowl. Pour the dressing over and toss gently.

Wash and dry the spinach, and place in a shallow serving bowl. Spoon the crab salad into the center, garnish with chili, and serve at once.          SERVES 4

**TOP:** Mung Bean & Basmati Rice Salad
**BOTTOM:** Oriental Crab Salad

# SALMON TERIYAKI SALAD

12 ounces skinless salmon fillet, sliced into strips
6-inch × 1-inch piece kombu seaweed, soaked in
cold water for 2 hours
3 tablespoons sesame oil
2 ounces daikon, peeled and cut into thin strips
2 ounces carrot, peeled and cut into thin strips
1 stalk celery, sliced diagonally
2 scallions, sliced diagonally
4 radishes, thinly sliced
2 ounces radicchio leaves

### TERIYAKI MARINADE

3 tablespoons shoyu soy sauce
3 tablespoons mirin
1 tablespoon superfine sugar
1 tablespoon sesame oil

### DRESSING

2 tablespoons sesame oil
2 tablespoons rice wine vinegar
1 tablespoon shoyu soy sauce
1 tablespoon mirin
Pinch of superfine sugar

Mix together the marinade ingredients. Add the salmon. Refrigerate for at least 1 hour. Place the dressing ingredients in a screw-topped jar and shake. Set aside.

Drain the soaked seaweed and cut into long strips. Heat 1 tablespoon of the sesame oil in a skillet and add the seaweed. Fry for 1 minute. Remove and cool. Transfer all the prepared vegetables to a bowl.

Heat half the remaining sesame oil in a skillet and add half the marinated salmon. Cook over a high heat for 2 minutes. Remove and repeat.

Wash and dry the radicchio, and divide between four plates. Pour the dressing over the prepared vegetables, toss, and divide between the plates with the salmon strips. Serve at once.     SERVES 4

# TOFU & ORIENTAL MUSHROOM SALAD

1 ounce dried shiitake mushrooms, soaked in boiling
water for 1 hour
¾ cup sliced oyster mushrooms
½ cup sliced flat field mushrooms
½ cup sliced button mushrooms
⅓ cup shredded fresh ginger root
2 tablespoons vegetable oil
2 tablespoons butter
¼ ounce arame seaweed, soaked in cold water
for 2 hours
1 scallion, cut into julienne strips
1 cup shredded Chinese cabbage
¼ cup sliced carrot
¼ cup alfalfa sprouts
1 tablespoon toasted sesame seeds

### DRESSING

½ cup silken tofu
1 tablespoon shoyu soy sauce
1 tablespoon mirin
1 tablespoon cider vinegar
2 teaspoons sesame oil
½ teaspoon dark brown sugar

Whisk the dressing ingredients and set aside.

Drain the soaked, dried mushrooms and cut in half. Place in a bowl with the other mushrooms and toss with the shredded ginger. Heat half the oil and butter in a skillet and sauté half the mushrooms over a high heat for 2 minutes. Remove and repeat.

Drain the soaked seaweed and place in a large bowl with the cooked mushrooms, scallion, Chinese cabbage, carrot, alfalfa sprouts and sesame seeds. Toss gently. Serve the salad at once with the dressing passed separately.   SERVES 2 AS A MAIN COURSE

**RIGHT:** Salmon Teriyaki Salad

## GADOH GADOH

3 cups peeled and diced potato
4 ounces thin green beans, cut into 1-inch lengths
1½ cups cubed fresh pineapple
1 cup diced cucumber
6 ounces daikon, peeled and cut into
thin matchsticks
1 cup fresh bean sprouts
1 cup finely shredded Chinese cabbage
½ cup finely shredded white cabbage
3 hard-boiled eggs, shelled and sliced
Oriental shrimp crackers
Cilantro sprigs, to garnish

### PEANUT SAUCE
1 stalk lemon grass, finely chopped
1 large clove garlic, chopped
2 shallots, chopped
1 large red chili, seeded and chopped
¼ teaspoon shrimp paste
2 tablespoons peanut oil
½ cup crunchy peanut butter
⅔ cup coconut milk
Juice of 1 lime
2 teaspoons brown sugar
1 teaspoon dark soy sauce

Place the first five ingredients for the peanut sauce in a food processor and blend to a smooth paste. Heat the oil in a saucepan, add the paste, and cook over a medium heat for about 5 minutes, stirring occasionally. Add the remaining sauce ingredients and cook, stirring, for a further 2-3 minutes. Set aside.

Boil the diced potato for about 8 minutes, until tender. Drain and refresh in cold water. Blanch the green beans for 1 minute. Drain and refresh in cold water. Place the potatoes, beans, pineapple, cucumber, daikon and bean sprouts in a bowl, and toss well to combine.

Line a shallow serving dish with the shredded cabbages. Pile the tossed vegetables into the center and spoon on the peanut sauce. Arrange the sliced egg and shrimp crackers on top, and garnish with cilantro. Serve at once. SERVES 4-6

## INDIAN SALAD

4 cups peeled and diced potatoes
1 cup frozen peas
2 tomatoes
1 small onion, thinly sliced
2 cups canned chickpeas, rinsed

### DRESSING
1 tablespoon vegetable oil
1 teaspoon ground cumin
1 teaspoon chili powder
2 teaspoons garam masala
4 tablespoons mayonnaise
4 tablespoons plain yogurt
1 teaspoon lemon juice
4 tablespoons mango chutney
Salt and ground black pepper

Prepare the dressing. Place the oil in a saucepan with the cumin, chili and garam masala, and cook over a gentle heat for 1 minute. Let cool slightly, then mix in a bowl with the remaining dressing ingredients.

Boil the potatoes for about 8 minutes, or until tender. Drain and refresh in cold water. Cook the peas according to the instructions on the package. Plunge the tomatoes into boiling water to loosen their skins; when cooled, peel skins, seed, and dice the flesh.

Place the vegetables and chickpeas in a bowl. Pour the dressing over, and toss well. Let stand for 1 hour before serving. SERVES 4

**RIGHT:** Gadoh Gadoh

## MOROCCAN LAMB & COUSCOUS SALAD

1 cup couscous
2 tablespoons olive oil
Salt and ground black pepper
5 ounces boneless, lean lamb, cubed
1 teaspoon ground cumin
½ teaspoon ground coriander
¼ teaspoon ground cinnamon
1 tablespoon chopped fresh mint
½ cup whole, toasted, blanched almonds
¼ cup diced dried apricots
½ red bell pepper, cored, seeded and diced
12 small black olives
2 tablespoons snipped fresh chives
1½ cups torn Romaine lettuce leaves
4 artichokes in oil, halved, to garnish

### DRESSING

2 tablespoons Greek-style yogurt
3 tablespoons olive oil
1 tablespoon lemon juice
2 tablespoons chopped fresh mint
¼ teaspoon ground cumin
Salt and ground black pepper

Place the couscous in a bowl and pour boiling water over to just cover. Set aside for 15 minutes. Fork the grains and stir in half the olive oil. Season well.

Place the lamb in a bowl and add the cumin, coriander, cinnamon and mint. Mix well to combine. Heat the remaining olive oil in a skillet and cook the spiced lamb over a high heat for about 5 minutes, stirring until cooked through. Remove and add to the couscous, along with the almonds, apricots, red bell pepper, olives, chives and seasoning.

Whisk the dressing ingredients in a bowl, pour over the salad, and toss gently. Serve the salad on a bed of lettuce, garnished with artichokes. SERVES 4-6

## CURRIED TURKEY & BULGHUR WHEAT SALAD

1⅓ cups bulghur wheat
2 tablespoons corn oil
2 small shallots, sliced
2 cloves garlic, crushed
2 tablespoons mild curry paste
1 pound turkey breast, sliced into strips
¼ cup raisins
1 cup diced cucumber
½ cup chopped Brazil nuts
2 tablespoons chopped fresh mint
2 tablespoons chopped fresh flat-leaf parsley
2 tablespoons lime juice
Salt and ground black pepper
Parsley and mint sprigs, to garnish

### DRESSING

4 tablespoons corn oil
2 tablespoons white wine vinegar
2 teaspoons mild curry paste
Pinch of sugar
Salt and ground black pepper

Place the bulghur in a bowl and pour boiling water over to cover. Leave for 40 minutes, until water is absorbed. Transfer to a clean linen towel and squeeze to remove excess moisture; place in a large bowl.

Heat the oil in a skillet, add the shallots, garlic and curry paste, and cook for 2 minutes. Stir in the turkey and cook for a further 5-6 minutes. Add to the bulghur wheat, along with the raisins, cucumber, Brazil nuts, chopped herbs, lime juice and seasoning.

Shake the dressing ingredients in a screw-topped jar. Pour over the salad. Toss well to coat, and serve at once, garnished with herb sprigs. SERVES 4-6

**TOP:** Curried Turkey & Bulghur Wheat Salad
**BOTTOM:** Moroccan Lamb & Couscous Salad

# FRUIT SALADS

Fruit salads make delicious desserts that are healthy and light, but you could also serve some of the recipes in this chapter for a special brunch or breakfast. Included here are salad recipes appropriate for each season of the year, from the light and fruity Red Summer Berry Salad to the stronger flavors of the Winter Fruit Salad, made with dried fruit, brandy and cinnamon.

## STRAWBERRY SALAD WITH PEPPERCORN & ORANGE SYRUP

1 cup superfine sugar
1½ cups fresh orange juice
Grated zest of 1 orange
2 teaspoons crushed pink peppercorns
1 teaspoon crushed black peppercorns
1 pound strawberries

Place the sugar in a saucepan, add the orange juice, and heat gently to dissolve the sugar. Bring the mixture to a boil and boil rapidly for 1-2 minutes, until slightly syrupy. Remove from the heat and stir in the grated zest and crushed peppercorns.

Hull and halve the strawberries. Place the strawberries in a serving bowl and pour the peppercorn syrup over the fruit. Stir gently to mix, cover, and chill for several hours before serving.     SERVES 4

## RED SUMMER BERRY SALAD

1 vanilla pod
1½ pounds red summer berries, such as strawberries, raspberries, red currants and loganberries
Strawberry leaves and flowers, to decorate
Macaroon cookies and whipped cream, to serve

### SUGAR SYRUP
½ cup granulated sugar
1¼ cups water

Make the sugar syrup by placing the sugar and water in a saucepan and heating gently to dissolve the sugar. Then increase the heat and boil the syrup for 5-6 minutes. Cool and set aside.

Split the vanilla pod in half lengthwise. Scrape out the soft center and stir it into the sugar syrup. Discard the pod. Let infuse for 2 hours.

Prepare the berries, removing stalks and hulling as necessary, and place in a serving bowl. Strain the vanilla sugar syrup over the berries and stir in gently. Cover and chill in the refrigerator.

To serve, decorate the chilled salad with strawberry leaves and flowers, and serve with macaroons and cream.     SERVES 4-6

**TOP:** Strawberry Salad
**BOTTOM:** Red Summer Berry Salad

# PEACH, BLUEBERRY & CHERRY FRUIT SALAD WITH KIRSCH

2 ripe peaches
I cup cherries
1½ cups blueberries
Juice of I lemon
6 tablespoons kirsch
¼ cup toasted slivered almonds
Borage flowers, to decorate (optional)
Vanilla ice cream, to serve (optional)

### SUGAR SYRUP
¼ cup granulated sugar
⅔ cup water

Prepare the sugar syrup as instructed on page 64. Set aside to cool.

Wash all the fruit. Halve and pit the peaches, and slice them thickly. Halve the cherries and remove the pits. Place the peaches, cherries and blueberries in a serving bowl.

Stir the lemon juice and kirsch into the sugar syrup, and pour over the prepared fruit. Stir gently, cover, and chill thoroughly. Just before serving, sprinkle the toasted almonds over the fruit salad and decorate with borage flowers. Serve at once with vanilla ice cream, if desired. SERVES 4

# THREE-MELON SALAD WITH MUSCAT WINE & HONEY

*Use a variety of melons of your choice for this fruit salad. The types suggested below make a colorful and delectable combination.*

1½ pounds watermelon
I pound cantaloupe
I pound honeydew melon
1¼ cups muscat wine
2 tablespoons clear honey
Grated zest of I lemon
Fresh marigold petals, to decorate (optional)

Using a melon baller, make melon balls with the three different melons. Place the prepared melon balls in a large serving bowl.

Mix together the wine, honey and lemon zest, and pour over the melon balls. Stir gently to mix, cover, and chill the salad for several hours. Just before serving, scatter a few marigold petals over the salad. SERVES 6

**RIGHT:** Peach, Blueberry & Cherry Fruit Salad

## CARIBBEAN FRUIT SALAD

1 large mango
½ medium pineapple
3 large oranges
2 large bananas
4 passion fruit
Grated zest and juice of 2 limes
6 tablespoons coconut rum
Prepared Sugar Syrup (see page 64)
4 tablespoons lightly toasted coconut flakes

Peel the mango and cut the flesh from the pit. Slice the flesh and place in a serving bowl.

Peel the pineapple, remove the core, and cut the fruit into chunks. Peel the oranges with a sharp knife, removing all the white pith, and cut between the membranes to produce sections. Add the pineapple and orange to the sliced mango.

Peel and slice the bananas, and halve the passion fruit. Add the bananas to the bowl of fruit, along with the pulp from the passion fruit.

Stir the lime juice and zest, and the rum, into the sugar syrup. Pour the syrup over the fruit, stir gently to mix, and chill. Just before serving, sprinkle the coconut flakes over the fruit salad.　　SERVES 6

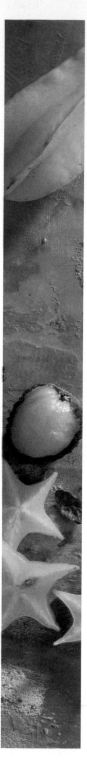

## TROPICAL FRUIT SALAD WITH LIME SYRUP

Prepared Sugar Syrup (see page 64)
Grated zest of 2 limes
Freshly squeezed juice of 3 limes
1 small mango
1 papaya
¼ medium pineapple
12 fresh rambutans or litchis
1 star fruit (carambola)
2 bananas
1 pound watermelon

Place the sugar syrup in a large serving bowl and stir in the lime zest and juice.

Peel the mango and cut the flesh into chunks. Peel and halve the papaya, remove seeds, and slice the flesh. Peel and core the pineapple, and slice the flesh. Peel the rambutans or litchis. Slice the star fruit and bananas, and cut the watermelon into small chunks.

Add the prepared fruit to the lime syrup and stir gently to mix. Chill thoroughly before serving.

SERVES 6

**TOP:** Caribbean Fruit Salad
**BOTTOM:** Tropical Fruit Salad

## RHUBARB, BANANA & APRICOT SALAD

1 pound rhubarb
½ cup superfine sugar
⅔ cup ginger wine
6 large, firm, ripe apricots, halved and pitted
2 tablespoons finely chopped ginger stems in syrup
2 small bananas, sliced
Greek yogurt or mascarpone cheese, to serve

Preheat the oven to 350°F. Wash the rhubarb and cut it diagonally into 1-inch lengths. Place in a shallow, flameproof dish, and stir in the sugar and ginger wine. Cover the dish and bake the rhubarb for 20 minutes.

Remove the rhubarb from the oven, add the apricots to the dish, and return to the oven for a further 15 minutes, until the rhubarb is soft but still holds its shape and the apricots are tender.

Using a slotted spoon, gently transfer the rhubarb and apricots to a serving dish. Stir in the sliced bananas. Strain the syrup from the flameproof dish into a jug, stir in the chopped ginger stems, and pour the syrup over the fruit fruit salad. Let the salad cool, then chill thoroughly before serving with Greek yogurt or mascarpone cheese. SERVES 4

## LOW-CALORIE CITRUS FRUIT SALAD

3 pink grapefruit
2 yellow grapefruit
6 tangerines
6 kumquats
Honey or maple syrup
Fresh lemon balm, to decorate

Using a sharp knife, peel a grapefruit, removing all the white pith. Holding the grapefruit over a bowl, to catch the juices, cut between the membranes of the fruit to produce sections. Squeeze any excess juice from the fruit membranes into the bowl. Discard membranes and repeat with all the grapefruit.

Peel the tangerines with a sharp knife, removing all the white pith, and slice the fruit thickly. Wash and thinly slice the kumquats.

Place the grapefruit sections, tangerine and kumquat slices in a serving bowl. Strain the reserved fruit juice and sweeten with a little honey or maple syrup to taste. Pour the juice over the fruit and chill the salad. Serve decorated with fresh lemon balm.

SERVES 4-6

**RIGHT:** Rhubarb, Banana & Apricot Salad

## GREEN FRUIT SALAD WITH MINT

Generous handful fresh mint leaves
Prepared Sugar Syrup (see page 64),
warmed slightly
2 tablespoons freshly squeezed lemon juice
1 large green apple
8 ounces green-fleshed melon, such as honeydew
4 kiwi fruit
1 cup seedless green grapes
Mint sprigs, to decorate

Wash the mint and chop coarsely. Add to the warmed sugar syrup, stir well, and leave to infuse for at least 2 hours. Then strain the syrup, discard the mint, and stir in the lemon juice. Pour the syrup into a serving bowl.

Wash the apple, remove the core, and slice thinly. Add the apple slices to the serving bowl with the mint sugar syrup.

Peel the melon and cut the flesh into small chunks. Peel and slice the kiwi fruit, and wash the grapes. Add the prepared fruit to the serving bowl. Stir gently to mix, cover, and chill the salad thoroughly. Just before serving, decorate the salad with fresh mint sprigs.

SERVES 4

## WINTER FRUIT SALAD

12 ounces mixed dried fruit, such as prunes, apple rings, peaches, pears and apricots
¼ cup brown sugar
Scant 2 cups Earl Grey tea
1 long strip orange zest
1 cinnamon stick, broken in half
5 cloves
3 tablespoons brandy
Mascarpone cheese or crème fraîche, to serve

Place all the ingredients for the fruit salad, except the brandy, in a saucepan. Bring to a boil, stirring occasionally. Reduce the heat, cover the pan, and simmer the fruit gently for 20-25 minutes, until tender. Stir the brandy into the salad. Serve the salad warm or chilled, with mascarpone cheese or crème fraîche.

SERVES 4

**TOP:** Green Fruit Salad with Mint
**BOTTOM:** Winter Fruit Salad

# SALAD DRESSINGS

Along with classic oil-and-vinegar-based dressings, such as the Italian Balsamic Dressing, this chapter features the creamy Blue Cheese Dressing and Guacamole Dressing, as well as unusual varieties, such as Watercress and Horseradish dressings. Use the lighter dressings for delicate leafy salads and the creamier alternatives for more hearty combination salads.

## ITALIAN BALSAMIC DRESSING

6 tablespoons extra virgin olive oil
2 tablespoons balsamic vinegar
I clove garlic, crushed
I small shallot, finely chopped
Sea salt and ground black pepper

Place all the dressing ingredients in a screw-topped jar and shake to mix thoroughly. Taste and adjust seasoning, if necessary, and store in the refrigerator until required. The dressing will keep well for several days and can be made in large quantities for convenience.
SERVES 4

*Variation: For a lighter dressing, use 3 tablespoons olive oil and 3 tablespoons sunflower or corn oil.*

## CLASSIC FRENCH DRESSING

6 tablespoons extra virgin olive oil, preferably French
2 tablespoons white wine vinegar
2 teaspoons Dijon mustard
½ teaspoon superfine sugar
2 small cloves garlic, crushed
Sea salt and ground black pepper

Place all the dressing ingredients in a screw-topped jar and shake to mix thoroughly. Taste and adjust seasoning, if necessary, and store in the refrigerator until required. The dressing will keep well for several days.
SERVES 4

## CHIFFONADE DRESSING

6 tablespoons extra virgin olive oil
2 tablespoons red wine vinegar
I teaspoon French dark mustard
½ teaspoon superfine sugar
I tablespoon chopped fresh parsley
I tablespoon snipped fresh chives
2 tablespoons finely chopped red bell pepper
I hard-boiled egg, shelled and finely chopped
Salt and ground black pepper

Place the oil, vinegar, mustard and sugar in a bowl, and whisk well to combine. Stir in the chopped herbs, red bell pepper and hard-boiled egg. Season the dressing to taste and use as required. The dressing is best used as soon as it is made.
SERVES 6

**TOP TO BOTTOM:** Italian Balsamic Dressing, Chiffonade Dressing, Classic French Dressing

# THOUSAND ISLAND DRESSING

4 tablespoons vegetable oil
4 tablespoons olive oil
4 tablespoons mayonnaise
2 tablespoons tomato ketchup
Juice of 1 orange
4 teaspoons lemon juice
4 teaspoons Worcestershire sauce
1 teaspoon dry mustard powder
1 teaspoon paprika
1 small shallot, finely chopped
1 large dill pickle, finely chopped
2 tablespoons chopped fresh parsley
Salt and ground black pepper

Place the first nine ingredients in a bowl, and whisk well until thoroughly combined and smooth. Stir in the remaining ingredients. Taste and adjust seasoning, if necessary, and refrigerate until required.

SERVES 4-6

*Variation: Substitute the tomato ketchup for 3 tablespoons sun-dried tomato paste.*

# BLUE CHEESE DRESSING

6 ounces soft blue cheese, such as Fourme d'Ambert
or blue Brie, stored at room temperature
3 tablespoons sour cream
2 tablespoons red wine vinegar
5 tablespoons sunflower oil
2 tablespoons water
1½ tablespoons chopped fresh thyme
Pinch of sugar
Salt and ground black pepper

Place the blue cheese in a bowl and mash to a paste. Place all the remaining ingredients in a separate bowl

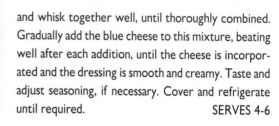

and whisk together well, until thoroughly combined. Gradually add the blue cheese to this mixture, beating well after each addition, until the cheese is incorporated and the dressing is smooth and creamy. Taste and adjust seasoning, if necessary. Cover and refrigerate until required.

SERVES 4-6

# GUACAMOLE DRESSING

*This dressing is excellent served with a simple crisp salad, as part of a Mexican meal.*

1 large, ripe avocado
Juice of 2 limes
4 tablespoons olive oil
2 tablespoons finely chopped red onion
½ large fresh red chili, seeded and finely chopped
2 tablespoons chopped fresh cilantro
Salt and ground black pepper

Peel and pit the avocado, and roughly chop the flesh. Place the avocado flesh in a food processor, add the lime juice and olive oil, and blend to produce a smooth paste. Season well and process again briefly.

Transfer the avocado mixture to a bowl and stir in the chopped onion, chili, and cilantro. If the dressing is too thick, add a little water. Taste and adjust seasoning, if necessary. Cover and refrigerate the dressing until required.

SERVES 4

**TOP TO BOTTOM:** Thousand Island Dressing,
Guacamole Dressing, Blue Cheese Dressing

## PEAR & WALNUT VINAIGRETTE

*This dressing is well-suited to salads that have blue or goat cheese as one of their ingredients.*

½ ripe pear
5 tablespoons walnut oil
2 tablespoons raspberry vinegar
Salt and ground black pepper
I tablespoon finely chopped walnuts

Peel and core the pear, and roughly chop the flesh. Place in a food processor with the oil and vinegar. Process briefly to produce a smooth dressing.

Transfer to a bowl and season to taste with salt and ground black pepper. Stir in the chopped walnuts, and use as required.          SERVES 6

## HORSERADISH DRESSING

*This dressing is ideal for beef salads and salads containing an oily fish, such as mackerel.*

4 tablespoons sunflower oil
4 tablespoons cider vinegar
I tablespoon grated horseradish
3 tablespoons sour cream
Salt and ground black pepper

Place the dressing ingredients in a bowl and whisk to combine. Taste and adjust seasoning, if necessary, and refrigerate until required.          SERVES 4

*Variation: Add I tablespoon very lightly whipped cream to produce a milder, creamy dressing.*

## WATERCRESS VINAIGRETTE

*This vinaigrette combines well with fish salads and it is also excellent when used to dress a new potato salad.*

2 ounces fresh watercress
½ teaspoon Dijon mustard
Salt and ground black pepper
⅔ cup extra virgin olive oil
3 tablespoons balsamic vinegar

Wash and dry the watercress. Remove any large, tough stalks and place the watercress in a food processor with the mustard and seasoning. Process briefly to chop up the watercress.

Pour the olive oil in a thin, steady stream into the food processor, with the motor running, to produce a thick, smooth dressing. Add the vinegar and process again briefly. Taste and adjust seasoning, if necessary, and refrigerate until required. This dressing will keep well for 2 days in the refrigerator.          SERVES 8

**TOP TO BOTTOM:** Watercress Vinaigrette, Horseradish Dressing, Pear & Walnut Vinaigrette

# INDEX